Pytl Programming For Beginners:

Python Programming Language Tutorial

By

Joseph Joyner

Table of Contents

Introduction 6

1. Inputting Python Data 9
2. All About Output 10
3. Python May Be Used as an Interpreter 11
4. Recognizing Numbers and Other Kinds of Data 12
5. Working with Boolean Values 13
6. Python Expressions 14
7. Understanding Python Operators 15
8. Tips on How to Work with Python Programming 16
9. How to Time a Python Function 18
10. Checking for Files Using Python 20
11. Optimizing Your Needs 22
12. Removing Brackets in Printing a List 24
13. About Generator Expressions 25
14. How to Determine if Your String Contains a Substring 26
15. Integer vs. Float Division 27
16. Python and Similarities with C 29
17. How to Avoid Loops 31
18. Conducting Lookups 33
19. Dealing with a Huge Chunk of Memory 34
20. All About Generator Expressions 35

21. Generating Outputs 36
Conclusion 38
Thank You Page 39

Python Programming For Beginners: Python Programming Language Tutorial

By Joseph Joyner

© Copyright 2014 Joseph Joyner

Reproduction or translation of any part of this work beyond that permitted by section 107 or 108 of the 1976 United States Copyright Act without permission of the copyright owner is unlawful. Requests for permission or further information should be addressed to the author.

This publication is designed to provide accurate and authoritative information in regard to the subject matter covered. This work is sold with the understanding that the publisher is not engaged in rendering legal, accounting, or other professional services. If legal advice or other expert assistance is required, the services of a competent professional person should be sought.

First Published, 2014

Printed in the United States of America

Introduction

Python is a programming language that is used for general purposes. It is described as a high-level programming scripting language but may also be put to use for non-scripting contexts. It is different from other programming languages since it embraces code readability and the ability to express programming language using only a few lines of codes. Python intents to create clearer programs for small programming uses as well as for complex and large scale programming use.

Python supports several programming concepts: it may be applied to object oriented programming, imperative-styles as well as functional programming. With the use of its dynamic system and automatic memory management features it can turn almost any kind of programming task a breeze. Learning Python always starts with the philosophies that are behind the programming language. Known as the aphorisms of Python, which may also be called as the core philosophies of the language, these basically summarize what Python programming is all about. In essence, Python supports philosophies that have been addressed by its creator and it is all about simplicity of design and ease of use. All these describe how Python is; it is dynamic as it is simple; it makes programming tasks easier without the hassles of long and complicated codes. Every aspect of the programming process is simplified and fairly easy to understand even by someone that will be programming for the first time. These aphorisms are described in detail in the "PEP 20" or the Zen of Python.

What is Python Programming for?

Python programming has so many uses and this is evident from its consistent high ranks as popular programming language. It is the 8th most popular according to TIOBE Programming Community Index and the 3rd most popular in programming languages that is not C based.

One of the basic uses of Python is scripting language for various web applications. It works with other applications to run a variety of web programs and applications such as Django, Flask, Pyramid, web2py and Tomato are to name a few. Python is used for data mapping, in communication programs between computers, cloud storage and so many more.

Python is also used in as a scripting language in developing software, as a language for scientific computing, 3D animation, video game development, creating artificial intelligence and in various natural language processing projects. Python is also used in the development of various applications in information security, software development for various computer projects and to replace Java in various office applications.

1. Inputting Python Data

There are two ways for Python to accept data from the user. Input and raw_input. These two are very different. Raw input is inputting data for Python to accept an argument or it may be used to retrieve a string of data as well. Input on the other had feature longer and more complex command string

Python has a file constructor and this is a tool in Python that can help users manage files. This built-in file manager can open files easily. If this is your first time to use Python then you will possibly find it hard to read the command but you may do so when read over the lines. In managing standard file objects there are built in file objects manager that may represent standard input and output as well as errors.

2. All About Output

There are many ways to generate output in Python and one of the tips uses the print statement in Python. The print statement will let users check the output with a clean and easier approach. Should you need to print a variety of things that are found on the same line, separate these objects or you may use a comma to separate them. There are more ways to define output in Python and it gets more complicated as the different words, characters and numbers become longer and increase in number.

Here are some output examples:

1) Print "Hi"

2) Print "Hi", "Folks" (it will separate two different words with a space)

3) Print "Hi", 34 (it will print elements of different data types and separate those with a space)

4) Print "Hi" + 34 (it will throw you an error as a result of trying to put together an integer and a string)

5) Print "Hi", (it will print a word "Hi" without a newline, but with a space at the end)

3. Python May Be Used as an Interpreter

Python programming is basic but versatile, it offers an easy way to interpret data by using simple commands. Similar to a calculator wherein the user inputs the information that he wants the program to answer Python can provide the answer using commands. There are ways to do this and it may differ from system to system. In a Linux or OS X you will be able to start doing this by typing the word `python` in a command. In Windows however this is already a part of the menu and therefore all you need is to access Python from the computer start up menu. Windows will open a command window or shell which is similar to using Python in Linux or OS X. A special integrated development for Python is called `IDLE` and this is used to make Python run as an interpreter. If you do not have `IDLE` you may download this online.

4. Recognizing Numbers and Other Kinds of Data

Python is so smart it can recognize tons of different kinds of data. Possibly the basic thing that you will learn is how the program can recognize a float or sometimes called floating point numbers. Python can easily determine what type of number (simple to complex numbers) and it uses suffixes to tell the users what the number is. For instance, Python uses the letter j after a number to tell the user that the number is complex.

Other than numbers, Python may also be able to recognize characters or sometimes referred to as data strings. Strings are mostly words or group of words that are enclosed in quotations (single or double quotations). Characters and numbers may be grouped together to create a list and tuples. Basic programming strings have lists that are enclosed in brackets. Tuples on the other hand are enclosed in a parenthesis.

5. Working with Boolean Values

Another important value or values that may be assessed using Python programming are Boolean values. This is a simple programming string that tells the user whether the value of a number is True or False. The Boolean type may be used to compare and to make decisions easily which is why it may be used on numbers or characters.

6. Python Expressions

These are not exactly commands; Python expressions are part of a command. The difference about expressions is that these produce a particular value. Expressions may contain different items such as variables, constants, operators and variable and function evaluations. You will find parenthesis and brackets in an expression and these help group operations and to facilitate the order of each expression.

7. Understanding Python Operators

You can find the most common binary operators in Python programming like addition, subtraction, multiplication and division. And just like in arithmetic you can count on the symbols +. -. * and / to represent addition, subtraction, multiplication and division respectively. What about numbers with exponents? There are two * or a ** near the number to mean that the number has an exponent. It is important to yield integers for a result and thus you should use integer division in your programming.

8. Tips on How to Work with Python Programming

Python programming is ideally for people that are learning programming for the first time however it may be easier if the user has previous computer programming background especially with the use of C programming language. Just like any language programming system, it takes time and effort to learn Python but after you have mastered using it you will be able to implement your programming skills into different tasks. There are a variety of techniques that could help you with your work with Python; here are some of helpful strategies that may help.

Be sure to install the latest Python programming language version

One of the most obvious tips that any aspiring Python professional programmer should follow is to download the latest version of Python. The latest for Windows version as well as the latest OS X and Linux versions may be downloaded from the Python website. Be sure to check out system requirements and information about the program to match your operating system. OS X and Linux already come with

Python installed. And along with installing the latest version you may also need to install a text editor.

A text editor will help you create Python programs easily instead of using only Notepad. Text editors come in various versions and the most popular are TextWrangler for Mac, Notepad ++ for Windows and the latest JEdit which may be used in any kind of system.

And aside from downloading text editing software, a dedicated Python user should consider continuous education and learning about new information about Python's features and possibly latest versions of the programming language. There are a lot of books, online articles, sites and programming tools that you could use to keep your leaning updated at no cost.

9. How to Time a Python Function

There are various time measurements in computing and the most common type is what we are all familiar of: execution time or CPU time this is descried as how much time a CPU spends on executing a command. Another type of time is appropriately called a wall clock time which is the total time it takes to execute a program in a particular computer; it may also be referred to as the elapsed time. The latter is often longer since the CPU may also be executing other instructions while it does the task. In Python there is a time module that is used in functions that need to be interpreted by time. A particular Python module is the `timeit` module that deals with the various behaviors of time in different platforms. In other platforms, the possibility of error is high but in Python, this error is non-existent plus `timeit` is simple to use for any kind of timing needs. `timeit` may be used on a Unix-based OS, on Windows and in IDLE. Another important use of timeit is that it can disable the garbage collector in an execution of a program. `timeit` is useful in so many applications this is why it is recommended as the ideal module in comparing different variables. In measuring a program's performance you should remember that your measurement should be always context-dependent so you may be able to assess the overall performance of a program instead of measuring only one aspect of a program.

There are various ways to time a Python function and `timeit` can do so in four arguments (`stmt, setup, timer and number`). `stmt` is the particular statement that you with to measure and it usually defaults to 'pass'. setup is used when you run the test before stmt again it defaults to 'pass'. timer is a timer object and number is the number of times that you wish to run the timer test. The `timeit.timeit()` function provides the number of second that the Python function was able to execute the provided codes. timeit may also be used to time a Python function with arguments and functions from another module. timeit saves a programmer time and effort to do benchmarking and it could also be efficient in various programs that require time-bounded activities and applications.

10. Checking for Files Using Python

Losing files is a problem across all platforms but Python has an ingenious way of checking if a file exists in a particular directory. One such way in Python is the use of the `os.path.islink(path)` wherein the function returns true when the path exists in a search. This is a simple command to use and will tell you if a file exists however what `os.path.islink(path)` does is that it can only tell if a path is a file but it will not provide information if the user may be able to access the file.

In os.access(path, mode) the user should have access or privileges to a given path. This will test not just if a file exists but also if it is readable and if a file is writable. By using the `os. R_OK` to check if a file may be read and command `os.W_OK` to find out if it may be writable. But even with the convenience of learning if the file is available and it may be written there is a narrow time frame between checking and accessing the file that it may be deleted or removed.

Any method that you wish to use to access a file and to learn some information about it may depend on so many factors. You can use any of these methods to save you time however os.path.isfile may work better. Each file access has its benefits and disadvantages so choose wisely.

11. Optimizing Your Needs

After using Python in programming you will constantly need to test your results however there are times that your program tends to slow down. The first time you notice the slowness of your program, check if it is still able to provide correct results and then run it again and see if it is still slow. Perform a comprehensive test to ensure that there is nothing wrong with the program ad that you can also point out which parts are consuming a lot of time to load. A comprehensive test will also ensure that if you make any changes or optimizations these will never affect the correctness of the program. Take this simple advice: get the program right, test it, if slow profile it once, optimise and then test again. By taking these simple steps you will be able to improve the program that you have created through Python especially the speed of your program.

Checking on the truthfulness of an object

Compared to other programming languages, you can immediately identify the truthfulness of an object. Python types are false if empty, and true if not. That means you do not have to deal with checking it out and wasting your time. For instance that the length of a string, tuple, list, or 0 or is equal to an empty one; it is often enough to just check the truthfulness of the object using Python easily. Of course the number zero is also false and all other numbers are true.

12. Removing Brackets in Printing a List

The trouble with lists is that they do not look great when printed, ugly brackets interfere with normal reading. It's of course obvious what the list is all about, and just about any user will never like to see untidy brackets around everything. If you would like to remove brackets then you may use an ingenious trick called the 'join' method. The join method turns the list into a string by placing items into a string and connecting them with the string where join was placed. The program is even smart enough avoid putting one after the last element.

```
favorite_foods = ['spaghetti', 'ice cream', 'donuts']
```

```
print 'The three favorite foods were: %s,' % ','.join(favorite_foods)
```

```
#prints 'The three most favorite foods are: spaghetti, ice cream, donuts.
```

As an additional tip, don't create a string by '+'ing list items together in a for loop. This makes the codes messy and it takes you so much time to do it. So stick with the join technique and you can be sure that you will get a list that connects and makes sense.

13. About Generator Expressions

Generator expressions function differently; these do not load the whole list into memory at once, but creates a 'generator object' wherein only one list element has to be loaded at a time depending on which one is needed. Of course you access one item at a time in a list and it is very rare that you actually need to *use* the entire list for something.

Generator expressions are described as having the same syntax as list comprehensions, however there are parentheses located around the outside instead of brackets. But if you may also want to use generator expressions for large numbers of items. List comprehensions may be used if you need the entire list at once for some reason. You may use expressions of the generator unless you are not able to do so, however you may not be able to find real difference in efficiency unless the list is very large.

Generator expressions must be surrounded by one set of parentheses. You only need one set of parentheses if you are calling a function with only one generator expression.

14. How to Determine if Your String Contains a Substring

You can test if a tuple, dict, or list contains an item simply by testing the expression 'item in list' or the expression 'item `not in` list'.

```
string = 'Hey there'  # True example

# string = 'So long'  # False example

if string.find('Hey') != -1:

    print 'Success!'
```

This is a cleaner and simpler version and it is using equivalent to do '`if` substring `in` string':

```
string = 'Hey there'  # True example

#string = 'So long'  # False example

if 'Hey' in string:

    print 'Success!'
```

15. Integer vs. Float Division

If you divide one integer by another, the result will be shortened into an integer. For example, performing 5/2 returns 2.

You may actually use two methods to correct this. The first and possibly the simplest way is to use float division wherein one of the integers is turned into a float. If the values are static, you can just add a .0 to one to make it a float: 5.0/2 returns 2.5. You may also cast one of the values: float(5) / 2 returns 2.5.

The results of floating is a cleaner code, but before you do this you must makes sure that none of your codes are depending on this short cut. You can do a `from __future__ import division` to allow Python to always use a float as the result of a division. But if you still need to use the truncating integer division, you can then use the // operator: 5//2 will always yeild 2.

1. 5/2   # Returns 2

2. 5.0/2   # Returns 2.5

3. float (5) /2   # Returns 2.5

4. 5//2   # Returns 2

5.

6. from_future-import division

7. 5/2   # Returns 2.5

8. 5.0/2   # Returns 2.5

9. float (5) /2   # Returns 2.5

10. 5//2   # Returns 2

16. Python and Similarities with C

Python will always be compared to C and this is not just done by professional programmers but also by people that are starting programming basics. C is most preferred because of its reliability but Python will be the choice for its readability. But what is more important is to consider how programming is done in the most efficient manner to be able to save time and effort as well as provide the most effective results.

So whether it is Python or C as a programming language of choice, it could actually depend on your programming needs. If you are looking for basic programming styles specifically for novice users then C is the best language to start but if you are fed up with long and messy codes then Python could be a better and more practical solution. Python is also a more versatile programming solution because it is open source and therefore you can do so many things with it. And just like C programming, a learner can devote his time to work on codes and techniques even more.

About algorithm changes

In many cases the greatest reductions in program running time is due to algorithm changes. That means that if you need to find a more suitable variable lookup then you should do so after you have settled on your program's algorithm.

17. How to Avoid Loops

In all instances you should avoid loops, especially loops that are nested ones. However there are still are some cases when your codes will need to have. But how to actually avoid loops; you should consider refactoring your code to be able to come up with a clean and simple code. Check out this simple example:

```
for x in a:
    for y in b:
        if x == y:
            yield (x,y)
```

do this:

```
return set (a) & set (b)
```

You may find that changes may not completely fit your algorithm. If this happens then you should modify your algorithm to accommodate the changes that you have made. For instance, it may produce less accurate results. If this happens, you should aim for returning more than you need, and then do a second review to remove the bad ones. The more time you spent reviewing your work will pay off in the end considering that there won't be room for errors any anymore.

18. Conducting Lookups

There are times when you spend so much time looking for something which could eventually cost you too much time and effort. If this is so then you may use a dictionary. If that is not a practical choice then you may use any other data-structure that fits your problem. For example, you are looking for search strings in a lot of files. You may create an index beforehand, and instead of looking at all the files each time you need to, all you need to do is to look at this index.

19. Dealing with a Huge Chunk of Memory

When dealing with large amounts of memory, the last thing in your mind is to reduce your memory requirements. A great idea is to consider an algorithm that requires O(n) memory, for n-sized inputs. There is also a special technique that may be used in writing your code in such a way as to use very little memory. This method will also enable you to write your code in a very efficient manner while using techniques to deal with memory issue. Your goal is to have as little of your data as you need available at any given time.

20. All About Generator Expressions

Generator expressions are used to list comprehensions. It is recommended that users take into account replacing such functions to a cleaner and more efficient programming string:

```
def myfunc(some_input):
    ...
    result = []
    for bla in foo:
        ...
        result.append(bar)
    return result
```

Here is a better and cleaner approach:

```
def myfunc9some_input):
    ...
    for bla in foo:
        ...
        yield bar
```

21. Generating Outputs

If your programming goal is to create output, you should dump it as soon as possible. You may apply this by checking out the following example:

```
for bar in myfunc():

    #process bar

    ...

    dump(foobar)
```

However you must ensure that the action that you will perform will not affect your data or you will not keep your data around for too long.

Possibly the most important technique in mastering Python Programming is to use it as often as you can. Since Python is very flexible, it is one of the best programs that you can use and practice even when you do not have any programming tasks to do. One efficient way to use Python is to do basic arithmetic tasks; Python has a basic calculator function or you may use the ** operator to signify the power that the number is raised. Python will calculate small to large values of numbers in no time at all. And you may also use this program in algebraic functions; Python may also be able to manipulate variables as well.

Conclusion

Python requires basic mathematical skills and algebraic skills however an aspiring programmer should take time to practice and get to know as many strategies, codes and tricks as possible to be able to use this programming language. It could be hard at first to be able to come up with even the simplest programming codes but as you test and tweak your codes you will be able to find out that Python is indeed the ideal program to use for people new to programming. By using clean and efficient codes, programming becomes easier to understand and to integrate in various applications. Considering Python in a variety of applications may be the best choice for any programmer.

Thank You Page

I want to personally thank you for reading my book. I hope you found information in this book useful and I would be very grateful if you could leave your honest review about this book. I certainly want to thank you in advance for doing this.

Lightning Source UK Ltd.
Milton Keynes UK
UKHW022100271020
372334UK00007B/828